FROM NEWCASTLE

Edited by Simon Harwin

First published in Great Britain in 2000 by
YOUNG WRITERS
Remus House,
Coltsfoot Drive,
Woodston,
Peterborough, PE2 9JX
Telephone (01733) 890066

Copyright Contributors 1999

HB ISBN 0 75431 786 2
SB ISBN 0 75431 787 0

FOREWORD

This year, the Young Writers' Future Voices competition proudly presents a showcase of the best poetic talent from over 42,000 up-and-coming writers nationwide.

Successful in continuing our aim of promoting writing and creativity in children, our regional anthologies give a vivid insight into the thoughts, emotions and experiences of today's younger generation, displaying their inventive writing in its originality.

The thought, effort, imagination and hard work put into each poem impressed us all and again the task of editing proved challenging due to the quality of entries received, but was nevertheless enjoyable. We hope you are as pleased as we are with the final selection and that you continue to enjoy *Future Voices From Newcastle* for many years to come.

CONTENTS

Killingworth Middle School

Sara Bull	86
Katie Johnston	87
Alex Pearson	87
Leon A Millar	88
Michael Oldham	89
Rebecca Allan	89
Ashleigh Donovan	90
Jonathan Cochrane	90
Emma Bryce	91
Lee Rutherford	91

Gosforth Central Middle School

Kimberley Sahni	92
Jessie Waugh	92
Kayleigh Slone & Nicola Elliott	92
Sabrina Bhalla	93
Richard Milburn & Paul Brown	93
Jack Bruce	93
Heather Slee	94
Philippa Leith	94
Laura Scott	95
Craig Wilson	96
Samantha Quearns	96
Kate Anderson	97
Mark Waite	97
Caroline McGreevy	98
Ahsan Shujaat	99
James Stephenson	100
Elizabeth Lawrence	100
Sarah Elliott	101
Freya Brown	101
Simon Beavers	102
Hollie Purves	102
Tom Somerville	103
Christine Blair	103
Peter Bloxsom	104
Fiona Urwin	105
Chris Foley	106

The Poems

SCHOOL!

I was very brave to start with,
I thought it wouldn't last,
My daily trips to Gosforth
Would soon be in the past.

My anguish when I realised
That trips to school would stay,
Maybe I had been naughty
And now I had to pay!

I sat alone at playtime
While others skipped and ran
I wished to be at home
Or sit and play with Gran.

The thing that came to haunt me
When I climbed into bed
Were thoughts of ravioli
Spinning around my head!

I know I used to worry
Of lunches dire and grim
What would they put before me,
To make my stomach swim?

I also used to worry
Of rules mayhap I'd break.
Of rules I knew not what of
Before it was too late.

Experience brings new knowledge
Which help fend off these fears
I'll tread the road with lighter step
For six more joyful years.

Emma Adams (12)
Central Newcastle High School

COTLEY

I can remember Cotley.
The forest; the green, quiet forest,
and the little brown dormouse,
scuttling through the tall trees.

As the coach stopped to refuel,
I could see the squirrels,
hopping from tree to tree.

It was a warm, sticky afternoon,
in early August.
Yes, it was a pleasant little village,
one small row of cottages,
and some shops.

There were buttercups, daisies,
and sweet bracken,
and the honeybees,
buzzing from one flower to another.
That warm, sticky afternoon.

Jessica Bradley (12)
Central Newcastle High School

THE KNIGHT

Shining armour, helmet feather,
Brave knight in stormy weather.
Silver shining moon reflects,
A bold knight on a quest.

Trusty steed to ride upon
Ready to go out and right the wrong,
Sword placed safely at this side
Baldrick and belt tightly tied.

Galloping away through the trees
Hair a-blown by the breeze.
Swiftly on and out of sight,
Silhouetted in the night.

Suzanna Fay (11)
Central Newcastle High School

FEAR

The curtain's up,
The play's begun,
I'm off stage,
Waiting, waiting.
My cue comes near,
I enter the stage,
Everyone stares,
Looks at me,
Waiting, waiting.
Is that my cue,
Or was that it?
My mind goes blank,
Then something clicks.
That was my cue,
My time is now,
I open my mouth,
Say my line.
Now it's over,
Now it's done,
I breathe once more,
I wait until,
Fear comes again.

Jenny Allen (12)
Central Newcastle High School

CAR JOURNEY

Are we there yet?
No! We just got in the car!
Are we there yet?
No! We've got to go quite far.
Are we there yet?
You only asked a second ago!
Are we there yet?
What? Obviously, no!
Are we there yet?
No! Just try and get some sleep.
Are we there yet?
I told you to start counting sheep!
Are we there yet?
What do you think?
Are we there yet?
No! Pass me that drink.
Are we there yet?
Yes! We're here!
So why haven't you stopped?
Why? Should I have?

Katie Brodie (12)
Central Newcastle High School

BEADNELL

Yes, I remember Beadnell -
Because, one afternoon,
The car pulled up for petrol,
And I woke up from sleep.

Someone moved in the shop,
My dad went to pay for petrol.
The car was silent, and all I saw
Was the name - Beadnell.

And the sea pounding on the rocks,
A ship sailing on the horizon,
The beautiful sands - empty,
As the waves moved up the beach.

Seagulls picked up the breadcrumbs,
A woman went to buy chips.
As my dad got back in the car,
I remembered the name - Beadnell.

Vicky Alderson (12)
Central Newcastle High School

COMMENTARY BY CARRIE COSGROVE

He's slain both dragons, two out of two,
Don't hang around, there's a damsel to rescue!
Climbs the tower, feeling brave,
He practically in evil's cave.
He's startled by a magnificent roar,
His white steed's being attacked by a wild boar!
Back down the stairs he leaps
But as he kills the pig, he hears the damsel weep;
'Good knight,' she cried. 'Woe is me!
For long I have wished for a husband-y!'
He rushes up the rickety staircase,
Running towards the beautiful face.
He'll make it in world record pace.
He reaches the door, not to be mocked,
Oh, darn, the door's locked!

Carrie Cosgrove (11)
Central Newcastle High School

WEREWOLF

A cool breeze
Blew through the tall, dark trees
Stirring the silver leaves
Casting dark shadows
In the pale moonlight
A creature crawled forward
Sniffing the crisp air tentatively
Ears pricked
Eyes gleaming
Its whole body quivering with anticipation
Suddenly
A twig snapped
Cutting the silence
Like a knife
The creature leapt forward
Eyes wild
Lips curled back
Revealing milk-white teeth
And blood-red gums.

Susie Hoogewerf-McComb (13)
Central Newcastle High School

DINNER TIME

Spilling out of classrooms, labs and the hall,
Thin girls, fat girls, the squat and the tall.
Running through the raindrops with bags over our head,
It's our school lunch break and we need to be fed.

Our school dinner's a culinary dream,
Red jelly with plastic whipped cream,
Burnt beef burgers with ketchup on top,
Curdled custard and cans of pop!

Friends in groups, huddled in pairs,
Whispering and jostling on corridors and stairs,
Friends in queues with weekend news,
Laughing and shouting with differing views.

Our school dinner's a culinary dream,
Red jelly with plastic whipped cream,
Burnt beefburgers with ketchup on top,
Curdled custard and cans of pop!

Emily Dolton (12)
Central Newcastle High School

FREE

The wind whistling
Round my bare feet
On the soft grass
Lifting my skirt
As I run
Free

A stream, cool
Flowing round my toes
Splashing my legs
As I run on
Free

A deep, clear pool
I dive
The water is soft
And comforting
Telling me
I am free.

Erika Freyr (12)
Central Newcastle High School

HIGH JUMPING ON SPORTS DAY

My heart beats fast,
As I run up to the bar.
Lift off . . .
I wait for the sound of the bar crashing down,
Silence!
I cleared it!

Again and again,
I jump the bar.
I must clear it,
My house depends on these fifty points.
Up and up,
The bar goes higher.

Slowly, people fail,
And at last,
Only two of us left.
She jumps and fails,
I jump and fail.
Just one more attempt.

My heart beats fast,
As I run up to the bar.
Lift off . . .
I wait for the sound of the bar crashing down,
Silence!
I won!

Alice Charnley (13)
Central Newcastle High School

THE ULTIMATE ENIGMA

Oblivion drowns reality,
numbed senses
intensify the pressure
as life unfurls its fury.

Comforts haunt the air
in reassurance of a kindness.

This is the End of the Beginning.
Surrounded by doubt,
it is feared by all.
Yet the victim
knows no such fear.

Dignified,
we all calmly enter
timeless existence.

This is the journey
to our final destination,
and the experience
of a lifetime.
But in human naiveté
we define such a destiny
as our End.

Stephanie Garnett (16)
Central Newcastle High School

THE DRAGON SLAYER

Riding through the trees one night
Came the most extravagant knight;
Shining armour, sharpened spear
Ready to fight, full of fear.

Then he heard an almighty sound
Unlike a human, horse or hound
From the inky dark-blue sky
Came a damsel's frightened cry.

A dark silhouette swooped down low,
What it was, he did not know.
A terrifying whoosh, a tremendous roar
Through the trees a dragon did soar.

With a booming, thumping sound
The dragon crashed to the ground.
The knight dismounted and ran forward
Ready for battle he drew his sword.

The dragon's skin, green as sage,
Took several blows delivered with rage.
As the battle came to a close
Fire blew from the dragon's nose.

The colourful flames licked the brave knight
Almost setting him alight.
Then blood flowed thick and red
As the knight chopped off the dragon's head.

As a perfect end to his heroic deed
Fair lady he carried off on his trusty steed!

Marie Franklin (11)
Central Newcastle High School

FIRE

The kindling flame burns,
Smothering the silence with a roar,
No one hears,
But the stinging heat tells all,
Rising, consuming all in its path,
A ravenous beast,
Destroying without mercy or shame,
Descending to hell.
Dark smoke rises, acrid and choking,
Funeral black,
And so it ends,
Ashes to ashes,
Dust to dust.

Helen Kelly (13)
Central Newcastle High School

THE MOON

In the deep, secretive sky the queen of the black cloak comes,
Her pearl-white aura lighting, showing the world below the way.

Like a pearl in an oyster, gold in the soil,
Her silent face shimmers, shines,
As she watches the distant crowd.

Yet gradually her glitter goes, her aura nothing but clouds,
Then the black soldier returns and covers the sun,
And the iridescent queen returns.

Sophie Slater (12)
Central Newcastle High School

WHAT IF . . . ?

What if the world was square
And you could fall off the edge of it?
What if cheese was green
And beans were yellow?

What if there was no suffering in the world,
Would it mean that no one would know what love is
As they would never have lost anyone?

What if computers, cars and mobile phones
Had never been invented?
How would we get around and communicate,
What would happen then?

What if money was no object to us
And no one scrambled for possessions?
What if we had no money at all,
How would we live?

What if there were no what ifs
In people's minds?
No one would say 'What if I had or what if I hadn't?'
Would there be no regrets?

Sarah Malcolm (13)
Central Newcastle High School

THE CALAMITY PLAY

It didn't start off badly,
But turned into a disaster,
Just to make matters worse,
In the front row sat the headmaster.

The angel Gabriel's wings fell off,
So did one king's crown,
Poor Mrs Barnes was in disgrace,
When the innkeeper fell down.

Joseph dropped the baby,
A wise man started to cry,
A shepherd waved his crook about,
And poked King Herod's eye.

Mrs Barnes was in a panic,
Her brow was hot and wet,
The parents didn't mind though,
It was a play they'd never forget.

Charlotte Pearson (12)
Central Newcastle High School

MY NEW SCHOOL

At quarter to nine I'm outside the gate
Being hurried along, trying not to be late.
Mum gives me a kiss and waves goodbye
But just as she leaves I start to cry!

I don't know where to go, I don't know what to do,
I'm ever so lonely! I hate being new!
I stand by the door, don't know where I should be
When a teacher comes past and notices me.

'Are you new, little girl?' I just stand there and cry.
I feel so upset, but I just don't know why!
The teacher repeats 'Are you new?' I say 'Yes'
She replies, 'I can tell by your lovely new dress!'

She picks up my bag and shows me around
I can see many children out in the playground
Now I'm off to my classroom to meet my new friends
I really hope this day never ends!

Rachael Lobb (13)
Central Newcastle High School

THE STORM

As the passengers leave the land,
And board their fate,
The waving hankies and shouts of farewell aren't scarce,
For the galleon is about to set sail,
Lots of hearts are beating like drums, frequent and loud.
Unsure of what the journey will bring,
Are all on the way to bed,
Sleep is easy on a rocky sea,
The galleon sails silently through the jet-black sky,
Like a cat looking for a mouse, it looks for a storm,
No sound is heard, not even a squeak,
While the passengers sleep in their cabins,
Unknowing of the danger which is nearing their ship,
Suddenly a ribbon of light sails through the air,
Defenceless to the power,
The galleon slips and slides,
Subsequently the galleon subsides into the sparkling sea,
Screaming people toss and turn,
Bodies freeze into the darkness,
The consequences of the storm are fatal,
As the galleon sinks all that is left is a *ripple*.

Bethany Lightley (12)
Central Newcastle High School

BACK AT SCHOOL

It's the first day of term today,
Oh what shall I do?
I've spent the holidays playing,
So, that's nothing new.

I haven't done my homework,
I've lost my swimming kit,
My shoes are still dirty,
My teacher will have a fit.

The holiday is over,
And I've had things my own way,
I've got some explaining to do,
I'm back at school today.

Kendal Spark (12)
Central Newcastle High School

CHOCOLATE YOGHURTS AND OTHER TREATS

'What have you got for lunch today?' said I
'Some sandwiches, lots of chocolate and a big apple pie,
Why, what do you have?' said Jane.
'Oh you know, the usual stuff, just the same.'
'What's the same? Let me guess:
Chocolate yoghurts and other treats?'
'Yeah, yeah, just that,' I replied
Then I turned from Jane and softly sighed.
You see I didn't have much to eat,
No chocolate yoghurts or other treats.
Instead I had a green apple and two crackerjacks
No other wholesome, delicious snacks.
Last night my mum was in a lazy mood
And forgot to buy the weekly food.
Mum said I had to make do with what I had
And that I should be grateful and also glad
That I at least had *something* to eat
And it didn't matter that it wasn't chocolate yoghurts or other treats.
I wish it was her sat right next to Jane
Compared to her's my lunch was worse than plain
'It'll soon be over,' I told myself
'And tomorrow I'll have the same lunch as everyone else.'

Nisha Joshi (12)
Central Newcastle High School

WHO IS SHE?

Who is she?
A maiden fair with beauty
Her gothic clothes all torn
Her pale, white face, her lips blood-red
Her hair black as midnight.

Who is she?
Gliding across the marshes
Brushing against the trees
Rustling in the bushes
Waiting patiently.

Who is she?
Crunching of the leaves
Footsteps drawing nearer
A tall handsome stranger
She welcomes into her arms.

Who is she?
A tender kiss of passion
A silent kiss of death
Her teeth pierce his neck
Draw blood hungrily.

Who is she?
She sucks the life from him
He falters and falls
Joins the undead
Forever hers.

Who is she?
The vampire lover
Together forever
A deathly partnership.

Sarah Hurst (13)
Central Newcastle High School

THE AGE OF CHIVALRY

The age of knights and chivalry,
And dragons is quite dead.
And yet the stories of their heroes,
Run about my head.

Great King Arthur,
And gentle Guinevere,
And gallant Sir Lancelot,
Who loved her so dear.

Wise old Merlin,
Who knows all but tells naught.
The knights of the Round Table,
The Holy Grail they sought.

St George slew the dragon,
Many years ago,
But his story lives on,
A genuine hero!

The age of knights and chivalry,
And dragons is quite dead,
And yet the stories of their heroes,
Still run about my head.

Olivia Potts (12)
Central Newcastle High School

UNTITLED

I come
silently
invisibly
a dark shadow
of sudden death
oblivion.

I am the dark
I bring the night with me.
I am the shadow
from which all nightmares come.
I was the primeval scream
of long ago.

I am as old as time
as dark as a black hole
as fast as light
as powerful as old age.
There is no escape
from my jet-black claws.

But without the dark
you cannot see the light
the day is nothing
without the dark
belief nothing
without doubt.

Ann Napier (12)
Central Newcastle High School

THE SURVIVOR AND THE HERO

The fierce, ferocious dragon,
Slumped down and died,
From the loss of blood,
Spilling from inside.
The dumbstruck damsel,
Fainted from distress,
Landed on a clump of rocks,
Cushioned by her dress.
The weary, kind dragon,
Lay down from exhaustion,
From rescuing the damsel,
And doing his portion.
The heroic knight,
Bounded in on his horse,
I know this is irrelevant,
But his name was Morse.
From the damsel,
There came a stir,
A few groans,
Then a huge *'Bleurrghh!'*
With her insides heaving,
She looked at the knight,
Stood up shaking,
And told him about the fight.
She walked over to the dragon,
And gave him a nudge,
Gave him a kiss also,
With lipstick all a-smudge.
The dragon chewed on a grass clod,
And slowly went off deeply into the land of nod.

Charis Younger (11)
Central Newcastle High School

FOOTBALL

I hate football, it really is a pain.
I hate football, especially in the rain.
Daft little men dribbling a ball,
What's the fascination?
I don't know.

There is loads of other things,
To spend your money on.
Apart from stupid football,
'What are they on?'

I hate football, I really don't know why.
I hate football, goodbye, goodbye, goodbye.

Andrew Jones (12)
Kenton School

FUTURE VOICES

Young people running around,
Laughing, playing, falling on the ground.
As they get older they become mature,
What job are they going to do? They're not sure.
When they leave school they'll get a job,
Teaching, farming or sailing a cob,
When it comes to election day,
Labour might win, they may.

Us, the children who make noises,
Are the future voices.

Kirsty Burrows (12)
Kenton School

THE FUTURE

The voice of the cockerel crows,
A sign the day begins.
The sun starts to show,
The birds flap their wings
Across the sky,
The millennium dawning
As they fly,
Above the parties of the morning.
The future lies in front of us
An open book, white and plain.
Will we still use the bus?
Taxi and train?
Murder could cease to be
Kidnapping and theft,
Also burglary
Could be left,
Behind us now forever,
In the past as we look ahead.
No crimes committed ever!
Just harmony instead.
The truth is no one will ever know
Will we be rich or poor?
Will business grow?
No one can be sure.
We shall only find
Our lives play out
As the stories unwind,
And the truth is about.
It is the only way.

Joanne Shields (12)
Kenton School

FUTURE VOICES

I hear voices distant to me,
People that I cannot see.
Then it takes me by surprise,
Images flash before my eyes.
I'm lost somewhere in outerspace,
With some vaguely human race.
I can see distant shapes,
Which are people evolving from apes.
Something's tugging at my arm,
I jerk away from any harm.
Then I open up my eyes,
And I get a great surprise.
It would now seem,
It was all a dream.

Alison Langley (13)
Kenton School

THE MILLENNIUM BEGINS

The fiery burning colourful sun dies out slowly
The horizon glowing, burning, blazing hot bright colours in the
                                        fiery sky hiding silent and still.
Above the tower blocks the silhouettes glow as the sun dies out,
Then the clouds sail away until another day.
Then Big Ben strikes twelve and the millennium begins.
The world goes wild when the New Year starts.
To others a thousand years ago this was the future,
But to us it is a celebration of a lifetime!

Lianne Allman (12)
Kenton School

FOOTBALL FAMILY

Dad's in goal
Granny's in defence,
Mam is a referee,
and Jonny's on the bench.

Daniel kicks off,
Kegg's on the ball,
Renton scores a goal,
and says 'I'm on a roll.'

My cousin is a dribbler,
he missed a penalty shot,
so he tried to be a goalie,
and missed the blooming lot.

The not then manager said he's useless,
he was going to give him the sack,
but along came the chairman,
and gave him a pat on the back.

Andrew Clegg (12)
Kenton School

THE TERRIBLE FUTURE

My grandparents tell me of the world as they knew it,
With healthy trees and pretty flowers, but cars that pollute it.

The houses and buildings are all now just rusting,
The rain is burning acid and the rivers are *disgusting.*

The memories of the beautiful globe are all dying,
The rates of pollution are basically flying.

Paul Blackburn (12)
Kenton School

I Think In The Future

I think in the future
The cars will be very fast
And that petrol engines
Will be a thing of the past.

I think in the future
There will be a car
That will go a thousand miles non-stop
Which is very, very far.

I think in the future
You will be able to shop over the net
You just have to press a button
And you will then get.

I think in the future
There will be a time machine
And the past will be relived
And the future will be seen.

Lee Curran (12)
Kenton School

Future Voices

Future voices,
Voicing speeches,
Speaking words,
Wording reaches
Reaches minds
Minding business
Busy thinking
Thoughts of the future.

Stephanie Henderson (12)
Kenton School

FUTURE VOICES

I think of the future
The future will be a better place
No hunger, no fighting, no pain
No countries going to war
No poor people
Pollution free
Children's voices and laughter
Making the world a happy place.
No more politics
Everyone living together, working together
Let us build a better world.

I hear voices in my head
They tell me time and time again
The future will be a better place.

Anthony Fatkin (11)
Kenton School

FUTURE VOICES

Will we all go to the moon?
Will we still be able to watch the Toon?
Will we still go to town on a really cold day?
Or will we find work with outrageous pay?
In school would you be allowed to make a sound?
And will the Brits still have the pound?
These are the things I'd like to know,
That is it, I've got to go!

Tal Kleiman (13)
Kenton School

FUTURE VOICES

Future voices are calling you,
Calling out to you,
Each little word they say,
Is a different word to you,
A different voice,
For a different word,
Each high or low,
Or old or new,
They put a word,
With another word,
To say something to you,
Maybe a story,
Maybe a song,
Guess you'll never know,
In the future
Listen very hard,
You might just hear
A little sound!

Lisa Atkinson (12)
Kenton School

FUTURE VOICES

The year is 2007
We're on our way to vote
Hey people listen to what we have to say
Take notice when we put our pens to paper
We've waited long enough
Now it's our chance to change what we think's wrong
To make a better place for each and everyone.

Laura Hunter (11)
Kenton School

BACK TO THE FUTURE

As we enter a new century,
There'll be changes we'll see,
Our future may be scary,
Or exciting for me.
Will I hire a robot,
Who will shop and cook,
Who'll make me a cuppa,
And read me a book?
Will I turn on TV,
And see Olympic aliens compete,
Or perhaps find one standing,
Next to me in the street?
Will I look to the sky,
And see a car with large wings,
Or maybe some other,
Strange and weird things?
I could arrive at a bus stop,
But I'm already there,
It's the cloning of people,
Same face and same hair.
Will I earn enough money,
For life's little pleasures?
A bacardi in a pub
£500 a measure.
I'll never get lonely,
With a dog that can talk,
Even feeds itself,
And goes for a walk.
So if this is the future,
Then there's nothing to fear,
It may sound confusing,
But one day will be clear!

Ashleigh Hutchinson (12)
Kenton School

FUTURE VOICES!

Every morning, when I wake up,
I wonder what the next day of school will be like,
The next day, or even my GCSEs day.

I wonder if my grades will be good,
Wonder if my children should
Come to this school,
Come to this very school, this very day.

And maybe my grandchildren
Will come too.
I hope it comes true, comes true,
My future voices come too.

They will speak for the world,
They will speak for themselves,
They will be the best scholars ever to be seen.
I hope it comes true, comes true,
I hope my future voices come true.

Stacey Baxter (11)
Kenton School

FUTURE

The future of the world is not looking good,
We are not looking after it as well as we should.
With all the chemicals released in the air,
People should start to take more care.

The ice cap is melting a little more each year,
The future is something we all need to fear.
Global warming is the cause of this plight,
But if we act now we can still put it right.

If everyone took just a little more care,
By binning their rubbish and cleaning the air,
The world would soon be a happier place,
And our future will be a pleasure to face.

Sarah Mooney (12)
Kenton School

FUTURE VOICES

The children are our future;
The future is in our hands
The future is our making
So start giving and stop taking.

The future will hold many faces,
And most of different races
Will we unite?
And stop the fights?
The consequences we will face.

The voices of the children that are ours,
Will bellow from the stars;
As they will soon
Be able to hear our voices on the moon.

The voices of the future will not be ours,
For we will be above the stars;
Some voices may be soft and mellow,
But other voices may be loud and may bellow.

So sleep light,
Don't get uptight
The future voices will be alright.

Chloe Cherry (11)
Kenton School

FUTURE VOICES

Our planet needs a revolution,
To help stop all its pollution.

Global warming has arrived,
So recycle all your waste,
Time is of the essence,
So we must make haste.

Peace is so important,
We do not need wars,
Negotiate your differences,
And have a get out clause.

Save the world for your children,
And all the human race,
Let's do it by ourselves,
And not by God's own grace.

Rebecca Emmerson (13)
Kenton School

THE FUTURE

Everything will change somewhere.
All the cars will be in the air.
There will be no more houses
And no more girls in pink blouses.
There will be blocks of flats
And lots of skinny unfed cats.
Everything will be ruled by computers
And the best job is a robot rebooter.
Is this the future for us?

Stephanie Law (11)
Kenton School

SPACE

Space! What is it?
Somewhere we thought we'd never visit,
For we have landed on the moon,
A colony could be built there soon.

Space goes on and on, to where?
Is there any intelligent life out there?
Have any aliens visited our Earth?
I think so, for what it's worth!

Only satellites have been to Mars,
Only satellites have touched other stars,
In the future this may change,
But to us, just now, this sounds strange.

Until then, it is in our dreams -
The thought of space travel and what it means.
I think it's safer to travel by bus,
Space! Is there any room for us?

Paul Crame (12)
Kenton School

MY FUTURE VOICES

Love animals; don't hurt them.
Don't hunt foxes just because some people call them 'vermin'.
We don't want any more dodo copycats.
Bullfighting: What's the point?
Don't experiment on animals; it's cruel.
Battery hens live all their lives in smaller areas than this page.
Now think about what I've just said.
Love animals; don't hurt them.

Ruth McCarty (12)
Kenton School

FUTURE VOICES

The future, what will it hold?
Living on the moon,
Has been told.

The millennium is to come,
Frightened,
Are just some.

New technology will arrive
Improving our lifestyle,
Causing businesses to thrive.

New style cars on our roads,
People gasping
At the sight of the new loads.

Fashion, it's changing all of the time,
What will it be like?
Will it be mine?

What will the government do?
Change to the Euro or
Change our language too?

People's dream homes will be made,
What about our houses today?
Will they just fade?

In the future robots will be teaching us,
Would people care?
They could even be driving the bus.

Will there be peace, will there be war?
Death and destruction,
What is in store?

Peace and hope is in my heart
So come on year 2000
Let it start!

Jilli Patterson (12)
Kenton School

THE FUTURE BATTLE

High in the hills,
Miniature robots with frilly frills.
Cruise missiles and nuclear bombs,
All seem as old as Vikings to the future squadron.

The future battle has now begun.
Sit back with a remote control,
Destroy your enemies,
Like in a video game
For the future battle has now begun.

No person gets hurt,
For the fighting is done,
By a robot and his laser gun.

But in 72 hours the battle runs short,
The batteries are dead.
Mount Everest is the highest point standing,
50 metres above the sea.

The ice caps have melted,
Land is gone,
The future battle has now begun.

Philip Watson (12)
Kenton School

FUTURE VOICES

The environment is fragile,
and very, very weak.
We are destroying it to pieces,
and soon it will go to sleep.

We need to look after it now,
or soon it will be dead.
This means with no environment
we soon shall rest our heads.

The next generation,
will have nowhere to go.
They'll live in indoor cities,
and there'll be nothing to show.

There'll be more pollution,
there'll be lots of pain.
There won't be parks or beaches,
or benches in the rain.

Kyle Smith (12)
Kenton School

FUTURE VOICES

In the year 2073
Where will we be?
Will people be living on the moon
Or will the world have ended with a boom?

Will scientists have discovered life on other planets
And will we see another comet?
Will aliens have landed
And will the queen have abdicated?

Will the hole in the ozone layer have widened
And will we have fried?
Will we have changed to the Euro?

Will we have flying cars?
Will we be living among the stars?
Where will we be in the year 2073
We'll have to wait and see!

Kimberley Strong (12)
Kenton School

BY THE YEAR 2999 . . .

In the year 1999 some people are excited,
hoping to see and share the new millennium with those closest.
And then there are people who think only of themselves,
and hurt each other on their way through life
but if we think this is bad listen to this,
by the time we are entering the year 2999,
everything will be *dead!*

People will have neglected the environment
and pollution will have become ridiculous.
People will have become greedy and demand money for everything
and murders will have become a normal way of life.

So come on people, let's make a choice
by the year 2999 we can join together
to prevent this from happening,
we can think of each other and of their feelings
to make the world a better place for everyone.
Together we can save the environment,
or together we can all be *dead!*

Bethan Williams (12)
Kenton School

OUR FUTURE VOICES

My future voice
will be loud and clear
about the subjects I despise
and those which I quite agree

My friend's future voice
is going to be cold
about the subjects she hates most
and those worth fighting for

Together our future voices
are going to be strong
and those who dare oppose
are in for more then they bargained for

People will fight
and people will win
and though the future is nigh
we will always win.

Cloe Lowery (12)
Kenton School

FUTURE VOICES

In a dark, dark place
In a dark, dark world
People waiting for the millennium

Now it is here!
People,
People,
Waiting for more.

When it's gone
They don't know what to do
Wait for the years to go on?
Or maybe wait
For the Armageddon.

Lee Clarke (11)
Kenton School

FUTURE VOICES

In the future there will be differences,
In the future there will be changes,
People earning more wages.
There will be new football teams,
Football teams with new strips,
But the manager, no more whips.

If I lived in the future I would
Get a time machine, then look at
The changes that had happened.
New TV programmes,
Maybe no TV.
I would take my friends with me,
So I wouldn't get bored,
Not my grandad though, he'd just snore.

I wonder what the future will hold?
Will there be aliens that are big and bold?

Will the world still be here,
Or will it change from a sphere?

I don't want to leave the world
It is so beautiful.

Marc Dummett (12)
Kenton School

MILLENNIUM

As Big Ben strikes twelve
This New Year's Eve
The nineteenth century ends
As the new millennium begins
Parties to plan
Friends to invite,
Children will be born on this special night.
A new life,
A new future,
I wonder what I will hold
Everything done by computers,
For young and for old.
In two thousand years,
Since life began
So much has changed
For the working man,
Breakthrough in new medicine
For the sick,
More help for the poor,
Shelter for the homeless,
These are some of the many things,
As the clock strikes twelve
I hope the new century brings.

Nicola Allen (12)
Kenton School

THE FUTURE

What will happen in the future? You'll have to wait and see.
Will you be the next English prime minister or could it just be me?
But the one thing I just can't deny,
Is global warming in the sky,
Will it come and conquer us all?
Will it stay or will it fall?
People, you must help me to try and save the Earth.
It's the only one we've got you know, it's only had one birth!

Global warming is a danger,
To this world's end,
So there's something you must learn
If you don't help the Earth,
It probably will burn!

The world is such a wonderful place,
I wonder why we spoil its face!

Candice Moore (12)
Kenton School

THE FUTURE

In the future I'd like to be a movie star,
I will drive a car,
A red BMW
It will be brand spanking new,
I'd live in Hollywood and meet the stars,
Go out with them for a drink in the bars,
We'll have a laugh, maybe be good friends,
Our fun will never end,
That's my dream but will it come true?
I don't think so, how about you?

Julie Hodgson (13)
Kenton School

FUTURE VOICES

My great grandfather fought in the First World War.
They said 'Tommy Brown's trounced Johnny Foreigner.'
His ears were riddled with bullets.
He never heard.

My grandfather fought in the Second World War.
They said 'Old Winston's shown off the Germans.'
His ears were lying apart.
He never heard.

My father fought in the Gulf War.
They said 'Uncle Sam's beaten Saddam.'
His ears were as radioactive as the rest of him.
He never heard.

I fought in the Frisian War.
They said 'Moral government's struck a blow against decadence.'
My ears were floating on the water, in ashy form.
I never heard.

Sam Ross (12)
Kenton School

FUTURE VOICES

A voice from the future is calling me,
it's warning me:
pollution, destruction, crime,
look out,
be careful,
because the future is near and the future is what you make it.

Philip Henderson (12)
Kenton School

FUTURE VOICES

I'm fast asleep after a very late night
When my mam comes in to switch on the light.
'Wake up,' she says, 'it's nearly eight,
Hurry up or you're going to be late.'
I turned round and said 'Do I have to go?'
And to my surprise my mother said 'No.
The way that you've been acting lately
You're gonna end up a lollipop lady.
You'll never have any good jobs to do,
If you don't always go to school.
You're gonna have to make up your mind,
And quickly, you don't have much time.
If you want to have choices about what you do
You've got to realise it's all up to you.'
My mother was right, I'd have to agree,
My stake in the future depended on me.

Alice Sanderson (12)
Kenton School

SPACE UP THERE

Space is a place
Up in the sky
I would like to go
Once in a while
But my mam says I am too young
I don't care
When I get older
I'm going up there!

Kimberly Rutherford (11)
Kenton School

THE FUTURE

In the future I want to sing
I will wear a wedding ring
Given to me by Michael Owen
For Liverpool he never stops scoring.

We will live in a villa
On the east coast of Spain,
We will get there in an aeroplane.

Everyone will envy me,
Will it happen?
Wait and see.

Lyndsay Sholder (12)
Kenton School

MY BEST FRIEND

My friend's cool
She's got the groove
She always makes me laugh
We sing together
We talk together
She's always there for me
We go to town
And hang around
I have so much fun with her
She's the best out of all the rest
Because she's my best friend.

Karen Foreman (12)
Killingworth Middle School

THE LEOPARD

I am a gentle hunter
Also king of the land

I put on my spotted robe
For when I go for my next victim

I'm only the fastest animal on earth
Also unstoppable

I crush the skull
With my giant teeth

When I kill
I split open the heart.

Alex Mawer (11)
Killingworth Middle School

WRITING A POEM

The page is blank with thin grey lines
Cold wind blowing on my neck
The classroom seems dead like no one can hear you or see you.
Now I've started to write, the page looks like the sun
With flames of grey lines.
When I read this out loud everyone's looking at me
Like beady-eyed cats ready to pounce.
Real poets work in offices
With their pens writing.
Poets are normally full of knowledge
All day and clever and thinking of lots.

Arron Hindmoor (11)
Killingworth Middle School

DOLPHINS

Dolphins jumping in and out
Out of the crystal blue sea
Playing and having so much fun
Swimming in groups of three.

Dolphins jumping in and out
Out of the crystal blue sea
Chasing the mermaids and the fish
Jumping around with glee.

Dolphins jumping in and out
Out of the crystal blue sea
Playing a game of hide and seek
The smile on their faces so happy.

Dolphins jumping in and out
Out of the crystal blue sea
But then the net drops and captures them all
They will never again be set free.

Laura Tate (11)
Killingworth Middle School

SPORTS

S ports are fun
P hysical and make you run
O lympic games are very sporty
P eople compete, get disqualified if naughty
R unners and all, fighting for prizes
T rying their best against all sizes
S ports are fun!

Jason Stobbs (13)
Killingworth Middle School

THE NET

Diving from the crystal blue sea,
Camouflaged against the pale grey sky.
So picturesque.
Splash down so suddenly,
Back to their deep home.
Chasing fish in and out of coves.
Then everything turns dark and perfectly still.
Fish stop bubbling,
Whales stop singing.
Darkness means silent fright.
A large net casts a black shadow.
All around animals turn,
Try to swim away.
Dolphins try to escape,
Not possible.
The monstrous net is raised,
That is the end of the dolphins.

Laura Usher (11)
Killingworth Middle School

IT'S RAINING ANIMALS

It's raining dogs
It's raining cats
It's raining again
But this time rats
It's raining mice
It tastes quite nice
I lick my lips 'mmm' sugar and spice.

Carmen Wood (12)
Killingworth Middle School

THE SHARK

In the deep of the ocean
The shark swims free
Gracefully gliding
Through the deep blue sea.

As it swims to the surface
You can see a fin
Look very close
And you may see him grin.

His teeth are all jagged
Sharp as a knife
If you get too close
You must swim for your life.

It searches for food
Through shipwrecks and reeds
The more fish it sees
The more it feeds.

As the sun goes down
Moonlight flickers on the waves
The shark dives down
To sleep in the caves.

Carl Johnson (11)
Killingworth Middle School

THE FILM STAR

Film star living life just for fun,
Make-up bill higher than Marilyn Manson
Wins BAFTAs, GRAMMYs even EMMYs,
Oscars they come two a penny.
Running up millions on the credit card,
Most of it on bodyguards.

Film stars thinking they're so great,
Staying out from eight till late,
Behind all the impurity,
Lies mental insecurity,
Unlike those they think they're above,
Film star, never been loved.

Mark Wardlaw (11)
Killingworth Middle School

WHAT I DREAM

Sometimes I dream about the stars and the moon,
Or other times I dream it will be Christmas soon,
I dream about the lovely blanket made of snow,
Where did it come from? Nobody knows.

I also dream about the birds in the trees,
I dream about the fish and the seas,
I dream about the dogs and the cats,
I dream about the hamsters and the rats.

I dream about the Christmas crackers,
I dream about the sound of maracas,
I dream about the cat on the wall,
I dream about the clock in the hall.

I dream about the trees swaying,
I dream about the children playing,
I dream about Santa's sleigh,
I also dream about him flying away.

I dream about my stocking on the wall,
I dream about the tree so tall,
I dream about the presents under the tree,
I dream about which ones are for me!

Carolyn Coatsworth (13)
Killingworth Middle School

GRANNY

I've got a granny
She loves to groove
She's so magnificent
She's got the moves
She's so trendy
And so bendy
But all her mates still call her Wendy
To other people she is known
As the granny with the flexy bones
She's so mental, kind and gentle
She'll do everything, anything central
She's reached the age when you must say
Have I thrown my life away?
Although I've lived my life with craze
Can I still go on living this crazy phase?

Emma Coates (13)
Killingworth Middle School

SHARK

S   idling through the water
H   overing round his prey
A   ttacks it
R   ather quickly
K   ills it sickly.

S   idling through the water
H   appily helping himself to
A   fishy menu
R   acking all the ocean
K   illing with hardly any motion.

Andrew Stockman (11)
Killingworth Middle School

SPORTS

Ice hockey is one great game,
I think football's such a shame.
Basketball is really cool,
Tennis really makes me drool.
Roller blading's really class,
Riding along very fast.
Cricket is quite a blast,
Ball hits you too hard - you'll need a cast.
But in my ratings croquet, comes last.

Mark Buchanan (11)
Killingworth Middle School

TO ME A FRIEND WOULD BE . . .

To me a friend would be
Someone who looks out for me,
Someone who makes me laugh,
And keeps me on the right path.
Who cheers me up when I am sad,
But sometimes makes me very mad.

Charlie Wallace (12)
Killingworth Middle School

PIGS

Pigs are pink and big and round,
they sniff along the muddy ground,
and when they see a nice soft spot,
they jump in with a happy plop.

Daniel Reid (12)
Killingworth Middle School

MY HAMSTER

He's round and furry, small and fat,
He lives in a cage away from the cat,
He runs around and around in his plastic wheel,
And when he stops it's time for his meal,
After eating his food he snuggles up in bed,
And soon he'll be ready for the next day ahead.

Darren Hoggart (12)
Killingworth Middle School

KITTEN

Kitten, kitten, oh so small,
You play with me all day long.
So small, so delicate, you fit in my palm,
You make me laugh when you walk.
You know there is always a place in my heart,
For you and your little walk.

Heather Jobling (11)
Killingworth Middle School

SHARK

Cutting through the water,
Like a piece of butter.
Eating all in sight,
With a big bite.
Chewing, crushing all he has caught,
So will he very soon.

Shane Sanderson (11)
Killingworth Middle School

WRESTLEMANIA

Ding, ding, ding, the bell rang
X-Paaccc the speakers sang
In he walked with his belt
He jumped in the ring, sat down and knelt
His opponent walked in down the aisle
He was the strongest by a mile
Austin, he was muscular and lean
All the fans chanted 3:16
X-Pac waited there to fight
He would use all of his courage and might
Off they went both eager to win
For they both wanted to be the real king
Austin went on with his mocking chants
And X-Pac wearing his black and red pants
Austin ran up *Kick Stunner!*
For X-Pac that was a real bummer!
Austin went up to get the pin,
One, two, three, he gets the win.

Daniel Bowditch (11)
Killingworth Middle School

WOLF

Running through the forest,
Like a hot knife through butter,
Stalking its prey
It catches it by surprise
No more rabbit.

Joe Amer (11)
Killingworth Middle School

CROCODILE

He slides down the mud bank,
All slim and sleek,
He doesn't raise an eye,
Not even to peek,
He sinks to the bottom,
Waiting to eat,
A fish comes swimming,
Straight past his feet.
Crunch! Crunch! Crunch!
He's just ate lunch!
He climbs up the mudbank,
All slim and sleek,
He doesn't raise an eye,
Not even to peek.

Daniel Wilson (11)
Killingworth Middle School

MY CHRISTMAS DAY

I can't wait because I'm so excited for my Christmas presents
The Christmas tree is all sparkling with flashing lights.

Then after my Christmas dinner,
I will get ready to go out to snow fight
And build a snowman with a carrot for a nose,
Buttons for a mouth and two pieces of coal for eyes
And my dad's scarf and I will use sticks for arms.

I can't wait for next year
So I do it all over again.

Raymond Brown (12)
Killingworth Middle School

THE BEACH

The golden sand and bright glistening water
The sunny sun, warm, beautiful and yellow
A yacht sails on the horizon so
Smooth, swift and calm, the sea laps upon the shore, swish
Swoosh, swish, swoosh, the sea covers
The sand leaving it soft and silky
A seagull flies overhead, hovers
Round and round looking for a bed
A boy jumps in the sea with a big fat splash
He gives off a giggle, a laugh of joy
He swims with his dog then he sinks like a log
He rises and swims still laughing with joy
A stone is thrown, it skims 1, 2, 3
Still going 4, 5, 6 then 7, 8, 9, 10 then sinks
The whipped up spray of the waves blows upon my face.

Paul Black (11)
Killingworth Middle School

MY CAT

My cat's so funny
He makes me laugh.
He spends lots of money
On Turkish baths.
He rides a bike on his way to school
Winking at girls (he's so cool)
I love my cat very much
But I wish I hadn't called him Butch,
When left alone he barks and howls
He watches Garfield and often growls.

Marc Morrow (12)
Killingworth Middle School

MY LUCK

I was walking down the road one day
When all of a sudden to my dismay
A great big bus came bombing down the road
I felt I was only three years old
For right before me a great big puddle
Oh no, I'm in a muddle.

Then before I could move
Splash!
I'm dripping from head to toe
Uh oh, people are coming, now I must go
Walking through the streets dripping wet
The mickey taking I must get.

But all this is for a reason
It's just my rotten *luck!*

Paul Wilkinson (13)
Killingworth Middle School

PARENTS' EVENINGS

I am waiting in the corridor, me, Mum and Dad,
I wonder if she will tell them that I have been really bad,
I wish I got my spellings right,
I have really got a pain,
The teacher stands there smiling saying come on in,
I hate parents' evenings,
I wish I had a brain.

Jordan Robinson (13)
Killingworth Middle School

LONELY DEATH

I know it's lonely when someone dies
But we just have to get on with our lives.

We think the world should certainly stop
Because everyone has to mourn and their spirits drop.

We think death is a big thing
But we could die from anything.

We were respectfully dressed in black
Then we saw a child at the back.

He will be all lonely from this day now
But his friends support him and not cause a row.

Rachel Hall (12)
Killingworth Middle School

AM I REALLY THAT MAD?

I love to do my homework,
It makes me feel so good,
I love to do just everything,
The teacher says I should.
I love to do my essays,
I do them every day,
Who are those men in white coats
Who are taking me away?

Stephanie Pullan (12)
Killingworth Middle School

YOUR HISTORY

History is what history was,
It makes itself, it wastes itself,
From past to present to future
'Cause history is what history was.

Past is myths, legends and tales,
Present is happening, now or never?
Future is depended, pretty or pale?
'Cause history is what history was.

From time to time think,
Could there be a missing link,
To this endless pace, that goes over in a wink?
'Cause history is what history was.

Imagination gathers around,
Those who do not know the cause,
From the evidence that remains unfound,
'Cause history is what history was.

Who, what, when and where?
History came upon those who beckon,
The reasons of doubt that make you wish you were there
'Cause history is what history was.

True time and time again,
You leave the same mysteries untold,
The past awaits to be unfolded,
'Cause history is what history was.

History is what history was,
You make it, you waste it,
You made the past, you are the present,
And you'll make the future,
Because you were history, you are history.

And history is what history was.

Daniel Doig (12)
Killingworth Middle School

HOLE IN ONE

Looking down at your golf ball,
taking a mighty big swing,
hits it with a satisfying noise, ping,
watch it go really, really high,
as well as going fantastically far,
look at it go, possibly a par,
there it goes and hits a bar,
a golf ball coming speeding fast back,
wow, it might hit your golf club rack,
here it comes sailing through the air,
whooshes past him by going through his hair,
there it goes, hitting a tree,
going towards the green,
your face, what a nice glean,
it starts to roll onto the green,
getting closer and closer each time,
he says 'That shot was almost fine.'
He looks at the golf ball,
where's it gone? Down the hole,
whoopee!

Ross Morrison (13)
Killingworth Middle School

ALL ON MY OWN

My dad says I'm getting big,
And can do so much now,
All on my own.

I can get washed and brush my teeth,
I can get dressed for school,
All on my own.

I'm on level three readers at school,
I can write my name and other words,
All on my own.

Sometimes I have to read to my teacher,
And sometimes to my mam,
All on my own.

I come in from school and make a drink,
Sometimes I help my mam make a cake,
All on my own.

I have a bedroom of my own,
I can play with my toys there,
All on my own.

It's nice to know I can go to the toilet
All on my own.

All night when I'm lying in bed,
I listen to the telly,
All on my own.

But sometimes it's nice to know people are close,
And I'm not really,
All on my own.

Jason Pearson (12)
Killingworth Middle School

Autumn, Autumn

Autumn, autumn, it's a funny time of year
When all of the leaves are falling
And winter nights are dawning
All of the kids don't come out to play
They stay in until another day
When all of the days are cool and calm
Mitts, hats and gloves keep us warm
I play out with my friends
Autumn, autumn, I don't want it to end
In the end it ends but I don't mind
I can stay in until another time.

Craig Ward (12)
Killingworth Middle School

Nothing To Do?

Nothing to do
Nothing to do
Put some mustard in your shoe,
Fill your pockets full of soot,
Drive a nail into your foot,
Put some sugar in your hair,
Roll some marbles down the stair,
Smear some jelly on the latch,
Go ahead and strike a match,
Pour some ink in Daddy's cap,
Now go upstairs and take a nap.

Sarah Foster (12)
Killingworth Middle School

I LIKE THE BEAUTIFUL ISLAND

The water laps across the sand,
Together we walk hand in hand,
The smell in the air could not get sweeter,
Me gusta mucho la isla bonita.
(Translation: I like the beautiful island.)

Orange glow from the sunset lights up the sky,
Birds sing in chorus alongside where they fly,
This is what you would call la dolce vita
Me gusta mucho la isla bonita.

Almost a silence but whispers in the breeze,
And the slow steady hum of the waves on the seas,
Nothing left of it now but I have memories,
Me gusta mucho es la isla para mi.
(Translation: I like it, it is the island for me.)

Lauren Laydon (12)
Killingworth Middle School

GUESS WHO?

I wake up every morning and see him on my wall,
He's got magnificent sea-blue eyes, but he's not very tall,
The way he talks is just so sweet,
He's the kind of person I'd really like to meet,
His first name begins with L, his last begins with D,
I am surprised you haven't guessed who it could possibly be,
In Titanic he played Jack Dawson,
The symbol of him is a scorpion,
Which means his star sign is Scorpio,
Yes it's really Leonardo DiCaprio!

Rachael Tumilty (13)
Killingworth Middle School

ON THE FIELD

Standing on the field
Watching the lads run by
Standing on the field
When they come past you must say 'Hi'

Standing on the field
'Will you go out with me?'
Standing on the field
He says 'Wait a minute I'll have to see'

Standing on the field
He says 'I've made up my mind, *yes*'
Standing on the field
I have to look my best

Standing on the field
Doing my make-up and hair
Standing on the field
I look and see him stare.

Fiona Barsby (11)
Killingworth Middle School

MY RABBIT

My rabbit is grey,
She is soft as hay.
She loves to play
She can hurry and scurry.
She is my rabbit Mopsy
She is very furry.

Toni Bolam (12)
Killingworth Middle School

DOGS

They bark sometimes,
They crawl sometimes,
They scratch sometimes,
They chase you sometimes,
They cry sometimes,
They growl sometimes,
They're little, furry and they're a bundle of fun,
They're dogs of course, have more than one,
No cats, no hamsters, no rabbits either,
No guinea pigs, cows or horses neither,
Dogs, just dogs, by themselves,
Like tins or jars on the shelves,
They can be little, or they can be big,
So many different breeds, they bury and they dig,
They're dogs, just dogs, beautiful dogs.

Liam Wood (12)
Killingworth Middle School

MY LITTLE BROTHER

My little brother
is good at breaking things
and being naughty at school
and thinks he's pretty cool
he doesn't eat his tea at night
and always tries to start a fight
when his friends come over for tea
he always tries to show off in front of me.

Nikki Rowell (12)
Killingworth Middle School

ARMY SOLDIER

Army soldier camouflaged in green,
Army soldier he awaits the attack,
Army soldier his gun in his hand,
Army soldier not wanting to use it.

He's scared of murdering an innocent foe,
Just serving his country like one alone.
But now it's too late because all of a sudden,
That innocent foe has given to you,
A first class pass to heaven with no return.

War we have,
We do not know why,
Wish it would go,
Wish it would die.

Army soldier covered in blood,
Army soldier not wanting to live,
Army soldier waited too long,
Army soldier no longer lives.

David Rayson (12)
Killingworth Middle School

FIREWORKS

Fireworks, fireworks in the sky
they might bang and they might fly
always stand five metres back
because it might give you a fright
so kids remember always treat fireworks night
so fireworks night will be safe and sound.

John Targar (11)
Killingworth Middle School

FOOTBALL CRAZY!

I joined a team to play soccer
We train very hard the pitch is chocka.
We're very keen and try our best,
To win games and beat the rest.
Alas our efforts have been in vain
Goodness me we've been beat again!
But we're not downcast
Some of us can run really fast.
We'll bounce back and win a game,
Teamwork and improvement is our aim.
Tim shouts at us to make a pass
And now and then we have a laugh.
We've realised it's not the winning,
But the taking part has us grinning.

Christopher Turton (12)
Killingworth Middle School

CASSIE MY FAITHFUL FRIEND

My faithful friend is black and tan with a shiny coat.
She has four legs and a tail,
She is anything but frail.
She loves to walk, run and play,
She also loves to have her own way.
With lots of hugs and strokes,
She likes coffee, I like toffee.
With big brown eyes she can get anything from me.
My faithful friend.

David Sears (12)
Killingworth Middle School

IT'S VERY BRIGHT AT NIGHT

It's very bright,
At night,
When you're at the speed of light,
In a school,
Next to a mule,
It's very bright,
At night,
When you're at the speed of light,
A future echo,
Of deco,
It's very bright,
At night,
When you're at the speed of light.

Gareth Nelson (12)
Killingworth Middle School

IN A TENT

I am in a tent with all my friends
All night long we have a laugh
We tell ghost stories that make you laugh
Then there is scratching on the tent
It's all right, it's only my brother
There is a light outside, what could it be?
It's only my mother with drink for all
After this we're all scared stiff
So we go back to sleep
What is this? It's my dad telling us to come inside
We're all relieved to be inside
Oh we're glad we're out of that tent.

Rebecca Hedley (12)
Killingworth Middle School

THE SEA

The sea is like a mighty hand,
Reaching out for the soft, soft sand.
The rocks are ragged,
The sand is gold,
You would not think they are so old.

The waves break on the rocks all day.
The noise, it takes your breath away.
In the day or in the night,
The sea can give such a fright.

Kings have tried to calm the tide,
By building dyke and dam,
But no man can,
Only Mother Nature knows the plan.

Jillian Reveley (12)
Killingworth Middle School

WHAT A FRIEND MEANS TO ME

A friend is someone who cares for me and who I care about,
A friend is someone who is nice to me and doesn't scream and shout,
Someone I can talk to when I'm feeling down
And laugh and share a joke with me when I haven't got a frown.

A friend will always help me with my ups and downs,
A friend will always stand by me against a pack of hounds,
Someone I can trust and share my secrets with
And rely upon undoubtedly without a hidden twist.

David Henry (12)
Killingworth Middle School

ALONE IN THE HOUSE

I'm all alone in my big house,
Mum's gone shopping,
Dad's still out.

There's creaking on the stairs,
Shadows on the wall,
And there's gentle tapping coming from the hall.
The wind is blowing through the letter box,
It's getting dark outside and the house
Seems so much bigger with me just inside.

There's a key turning in the lock,
Who could it be?
A monster from Mars?
Or even a burglar trying to get me?

I don't wait to see,
I jump behind the couch,
A shadow enters the room,
The lights go on,
And I look up to see . . .
My mum smiling at me!

Kate Proudlock (12)
Killingworth Middle School

THE OLD DOG

He runs along the muddy grass,
He's really running very fast,
He hits a stone and tumbles over,
Now he knows his time is over.

James Tiplady (11)
Killingworth Middle School

I WISH I HAD A HORSE

The unicorn sings,
As I say my prayers,
I wish I had a horse,
To love for and care.

I plead with my mum,
She sings me to sleep,
I plead with my dad,
He says not to weep.

I wish I had a horse,
To love for and care,
It all started one morning,
When I saw that mare.

She whinnied to me,
As I calmly walked past,
I couldn't help but stop,
And stroke her fair locks,
And well . . . I guess it all started from there.

I wish I had a horse,
To love for and care,
Maybe a gelding,
Or maybe a cob,
But mostly an Arab,
Just like that mare . . .
The one I love the most.

Ashley Whitehill (12)
Killingworth Middle School

ANGELS

I can see you behind that cloud
With those delicate wings you should be proud
With that halo, upon your head
You'd never think that you were dead
What a wonderful angel you are being
I can't believe what I am seeing
What's it like living up there?
Those golden gates I can't help but stare
I'm the back on the ground looking up at the sky
Thinking to myself, 'Why oh why?'
Why do I think these mysterious thoughts?
Why can't I just play on the tennis courts
I enjoy lying on my back all of the day
And that's the way I want it to stay.

Katy Macleod (12)
Killingworth Middle School

RABBITS

Rabbits are cute and cuddly
They are lovely and snugly
They are warm, loving and caring
But they are not really good at sharing
Rabbits, rabbits are the best
Even when they're at rest
Rabbits run free like
You and me.

Samantha Lee (11)
Killingworth Middle School

TIGER MY DOG

Tiger, tiger burning bright,
Tiger, tiger in the night,
Tiger, tiger can't sleep,
Have you tried counting sheep?
Why do you growl,
When you see an owl?
Why do you cry when,
We won't let you out?
I've so many questions to ask,
And when I come in the door,
You always pounce and lick my face,
With your dog food breath,
But really you love me so and,
I love you even more.

Victoria Hull (12)
Killingworth Middle School

THE KESTREL'S FLIGHT

Hovering in the cold.
Looking down on secrets untold.
He hurtles down onto his prey.
Horrible but that's the kestrel's way.
Carrying his food into the air,
This is terribly unfair.
Kestrels are amazing birds,
They use no words,
These birds only use a cry,
But nobody understands why.

Iain Taylor (11)
Killingworth Middle School

KIDS WILL RULE

When kids will rule,
There'll be no school.
No politics, no money, just fun.
A simple life with plenty of spice,
And humour for everyone.

Humongous rides,
And slippery slides,
And popcorn, and cola, and gum,
With lots of pleasure,
And plenty to quench a
Really, really, really bad thirst.

No Tony Blair,
No reason to care,
No laws, no rules, no government fools.
Hide and seek, parents can't speak,
Watch out! This is the future for us, (someday).

Jonathan Reay (12)
Killingworth Middle School

PLAYING POEM

Playing in the play yard,
Playing in the street,
Playing with the basketball
In between your feet.
Playing in the garden,
Playing in the house,
Playing with the dollies
And the mouse.

Elizabeth Robinson (12)
Killingworth Middle School

THE NIGHT

I lie awake in my bed,
Thinking of the day ahead.
I close my eyes, I can't sleep
I've even tried counting sheep.
I look out of my window, what do I see?
Two large eyes staring at me.
I shiver and shake, what could it be?
Phew, it's only my cat looking at me.
I lie back down and try to sleep
But there's a shadow at my feet.
It's tall and big and rather thin,
It's only Dad come to tuck me in.
'Goodnight sweetheart,' he said to me
'Close your eyes and count to three,
You'll soon nod off, trust me.'

Jade McNamara (12)
Killingworth Middle School

I AM

A sparkly, fuzzy photo frame,
a Statue of Liberty all lit up at night,
a white and black, elegant unicorn,
a slice of chocolate cake with chocolate icing
also with hundreds and thousands on top
with a dollop of vanilla ice-cream,
a part of a bouncing Steps single with exciting sounds,
an exciting, funny, winding, twining poem,
a trickling, slow, tinkly, sparkly river,
I am.

Amie Foreman (12)
Killingworth Middle School

BOYS!

Boys are not cool,
They think that they rule.
They splash you with water,
They cover you in mud,
They don't say sorry,
When they really should.

Boys love to kick,
Punch and push,
When a girl walks past they say
'Oh, isn't she lush!'

Boys love tennis, cricket, rugby and all,
But most of them are crazy about football.

Love them, hate them,
Can't stand the noise.
But whatever we think,
Boys will be boys.

Danielle Boustead (12)
Killingworth Middle School

SM: TV LIVE

SM: TV live
Starts at 9:25
I get up at ten
And I miss it
Once again.

Veronica Foster (11)
Killingworth Middle School

DOOMSDAY

I see the light,
At the end of the tunnel.
I see the sky,
It's filled with stars.
In twelve hours time,
My life will end.
The ground I walk on,
Will smash into billions of pieces.
Jupiter is getting closer,
You can see it now in the sky,
You can almost reach out and touch it.
Six hours left and counting.
Doomsday approaches closer and closer.
The world's in a panic,
Three hours and counting.
The streets are bare,
People are waiting,
To meet their fate.
I close the book
And look up,
One day maybe.

James Cruddas (13)
Killingworth Middle School

HAMSTER

Hamsters are so small
Sitting in your hand
Crawling about
Rolling away from you.

Sitting in its cage
Playing in its wheel
Sitting in its food bowl
Filling up its mouth for food.

Sleeping through the day
Keeps you awake all night
But still very cuddly
And very, very nice.

Sarah-Jayne Morrison (11)
Killingworth Middle School

THERE WAS A ROBOT

There was a robot from space
Who had a silver steel face.
He was rusty and old
And he was totally bald
Plus he is a lot like the human race.

There was a robot called Jim
His body was shaped like a tin.
He had extending arms
These were his lucky charms
And he lived in a portable bin.

There was a robot made of steel
Screws were his favourite meal.
With bolts as seconds
But screws he beckons
He ate them to help him heal.

There was a robot that liked to drink oil
But after a while it took its toil.
Because oil to robots is like beer
And in the end it cost him dear
Death even he could not foil.

Richard Clark (12)
Killingworth Middle School

THE LION

I'm the king of the jungle,
The mightiest in the forest,
I roar but never mumble.

Anybody who challenges me,
If anyone would that is,
They will end up in my belly.

I can kill anything,
If I really want to,
Which proves I am the king.

At night I really come alive,
Playing with my family,
Ducking when my children dive.

Then I sleep,
Peace at last,
From the jungle not a peep.

Daniel Bradford (12)
Killingworth Middle School

SHOPPING SALE

Hey I'm a shopkeeper and I've got news for you,
So don't just sit at home and think of what to do,
Get down to my shop and have a look through,
Get down to my shop 'cause I've got stuff for you,
If you get down quick I'll put on my sale,
If you sit and wait your shopping luck will fail,
So come on, hurry up and get down to my shopping sale.

Gayle Jamieson (11)
Killingworth Middle School

HORSES, HORSES

Horses, horses,
galloping around,
bucking and rearing as they go.

Attractive stallions,
with their wild forelock and tail,
canter around and run away,
from the people nearby.

Horses, horses,
see them here,
see them there,
see them everywhere,
horses, horses.

Carina Curn (11)
Killingworth Middle School

CHEETAH

I am a hunter in the night
Pouncing on whatever comes into my sight.

I hunt to help my family live
Also so that we don't grow skinny and thin.

I run like the wind so that no one can catch me
Not even man if I lived in the country.

I camouflage well with my surroundings
As long as I'm still they will never find me.

Now I return back to my home with a smile on my face
Which no one can change not even if I begin to pace.

Amanda Dyne (11)
Killingworth Middle School

RABBITS

A rabbit is bouncy,
it's a bundle of fun.
It leaps around
in the warm, summer sun.

A rabbit's always happy,
it looks like it's smiling.
One thing you'll never see
is a rabbit crying.

Rabbits are colourful creatures,
they're grey, black, white or even brown.
My favourite animal story
is a book called Watership Down.

I'd like a rabbit for Christmas
but I'd really like one now.
Maybe I'll get one
someday, somehow.

Helen Steljes (11)
Killingworth Middle School

EQUINE GOOD LOOKS

Roger, Roger, he's my horse
He comes first in the jumping course.
Looks so great and is handsome,
Trots along joyfully prancing
14 hands above the rest.

Maria McFarlane (12)
Killingworth Middle School

PICNIC HAIKU

The sun is shining
what a great, wonderful day
let's have a picnic

Sitting having lunch
a bunch of army ants came too
then the birds and bees

We sat up a tree
a beautiful bear we see
we're digging in now

We are packing up
time to go home everyone
we are on our way

Stuart Thompson (11)
Killingworth Middle School

TEACHER

Miss, Miss, can I go to the toilet?
Miss, Miss, what do I do next?

Stuck in a classroom
I wish I was in a bathroom

Everyday stress
Is just enough mess

For everything to go wrong
When the bell goes bong

The rush hour has just begun.

Helen Cryer (11)
Killingworth Middle School

MY HAIKU ABOUT THE COUNTRYSIDE

The country is grand
They don't have giant damns.
Lots of horses
A big tractor in the field
A tiny calf being born.

Sheep being sheared
Cars chugging along the road
A dog chasing sheep
A child's laughing in the field
Mice eating red berries.

A cow goes moo, moo
People in the sea swimming
Farmer shearing sheep
Crows in the field steeling food
People eating ice-cream.

Jemma Beveridge (11)
Killingworth Middle School

SPACE IS ALL AROUND US

Space is all around us
You can never get rid of it
There're planets of fire and stars that shine
There're UFOs, unbeatable defence systems
Space is all around us
You can never get rid of it
There's black holes and monsters that shove and haul
The noise is so great you'll shake all over
Space is all around us.

Luke Skelton (12)
Killingworth Middle School

A Poem About Writing A Poem

The page is blank
White as snow
Like your mind
Before you write your first line
Once you've done that, your knowledge spills out
All over the page in a flurry of words.

The blue writing on the page is like a spider covered in ink
Dancing all over the page
Spinning inky webs.

Oh no! I've got to read this out in front of the class!
How embarrassing
It's like everyone knowing what you're thinking

Phew, I'm finished
Wow, that was hard
Oh well, it's not so embarrassing after all.

Spencer Patchett (11)
Killingworth Middle School

Why Me?

Got to school right on time,
Bullying started right in the line,
Pushing and shoving,
Nipping and kicking,
Why me? I ask myself,
Why me?
Nobody notices it's plain to see,
Please somebody will you help me?

Natalie Tate (12)
Killingworth Middle School

SEASONS

S   pring when baby animals are born,
P   lenty of crops in the field, farmers growing corn.
R   abbits and animals come out from their sleep,
I   n the springtime lambs are had by sheep.
N   ow that will tell you something about spring.
G   rass and animals and everything else it will bring.

S   ummer is the season of fun
U   mbrellas are only used as shade from the sun.
M   y holidays are good, because you can get tanned,
M   ake sandcastles on the beach with lots of sand.
E   ach day of the holidays is really great,
R   emember school's coming (that's the bit I hate).

A   ll Hallows Eve is a fun time in autumn,
U   mbrellas are used more and fireworks you've bought 'em.
T   hey shoot up into the sky,
U   p they go really high
M   aking a noise and making a sound
N   ow be careful when they hit the ground.

W   inter, a season of the year,
I   t is full of Christmas cheer,
N   o one's going swimming, 'cause outside there's snow,
T   he children are all saying ho, ho, ho
E   ach present is opened, and each one is dear,
R   emember after Christmas have a Happy New Year.

Jenny Burns (11)
Killingworth Middle School

CHAOS!

First of all there's my mum and dad
telling me off for doing something bad.
Then it's my gran
getting cooled off by the electric fan.
Then it's my aunty and uncle sitting around
reading the newspaper very loud.
Then it's my sisters and brothers knocking the lampshade down
playing blind man's buff with a frown.
There's also my cousins running around
putting pizza and chocolate in their mouths.
There's my nana and grandad walking in the front door
looking outstanding from head to toe,
that's when the fun really began.

Charlotte Winspear (12)
Killingworth Middle School

SPACE, THE FINAL FRONTIER

Space, the final frontier.

Red-hot Mercury with its boiling atmosphere.
Cloudy Venus with its electrifying skies.
Fertile Earth with its blue seas and green lands.
Red baron Mars with its deep craters and extinct volcanoes.
Fiery Jupiter with its flaming storms and blistering heat.
Dusty Saturn with its beautiful rings and many empty moons.
Green empty Uranus with its icy moons and diagonal rings.
Very blue Neptune with its watery surface and perfectly flat rings.
And last of all tiny Pluto with its dull grey surface on one lonely orbit.

Space, it's the final frontier.

Iain Surgey (12)
Killingworth Middle School

ISLAND

I sit here alone
On a desert island
Far away in the sun
The palm trees are swaying
The coconuts fall
Down, down, down
The trees are that tall
It's peaceful here on my island
The bright sun shines warmly
Tanning my skin
The waves crash around splashing
Onto the beach
It's nice to be here so far out of reach
It's night time now, the sun has gone down
The moon casts its shadows
It's time to lie down.

Callum Colback (12)
Killingworth Middle School

TEENAGERS

As you become a teenager,
Lots of things occur,
Like spots and fashion and hairstyle,
Which all make life worse,
Boys become pests,
Which makes your life a mess,
So don't become a teenager,
Until you know the rest.

Jessika Rowell (12)
Killingworth Middle School

A DOG CALLED JENGA

Like a tower of carefully balanced blocks
Jenga can make the table rock
A German Shepherd, black and gold
Loved dearly, will never be sold.

Plenty of exercise daily is needed
He chases his ball till with sweat he is beaded.
From him I hide expensive footballs
Or he will pop them before you can call.

Tail chasing around, around
Until he falls heavily to the ground
Jenga and Stephen, best of mates
We'll share the food from off our plates.

Stephen Cook (12)
Killingworth Middle School

GROOVY POPSTARS

Hey you groovy popstars
have you all got funky cars?
Your groovy shoes and groovy clothes
all look good for a groovy pose.
Your music's great
and not too late.
Your concerts are fun
special occasion nobody would shun.
So it's bye from me
soon you'll see
what life would be
without me.

Leanne Wright (12)
Killingworth Middle School

INNOCENT!

Leave me alone,
I'm innocent I tell you,
You got my mother,
My father, and even my brother.

Leave me alone,
I'm innocent I tell you,
Don't kill me,
Just for your pleasure.

Leave me alone,
I'm innocent I tell you,
I'm just a little fox,
A little innocent one.
Please don't kill me,
I've done nothing wrong.

Lucy Abbott (12)
Killingworth Middle School

IMAGINE A WORLD

Can you imagine a world without love?
Love's like heaven high above
Love can be with anyone
As with it your life's a song.

Imagine a world without love
It would be like Noah without his dove
Love can blossom anywhere
As love is there to share.

Imagine a world without someone to hold
That world would be dark and cold.

Sara Bull (12)
Killingworth Middle School

PARTY ON!

It's a groovy party
lots of fun and noise
it's a groovy party
for all the girls and boys.

Balloons and streamers everywhere
girls with glitter in their hair
boys are drinking lots of punch
what a rowdy, noisy bunch.

Fun and laughter all around
dancing, singing to the sound
lights flashing bright and fast
the party's over very fast.

The olds are home
I'm just in time
I've wiped away the last bit of grime.
It's over now but not for long
they're out on Friday, *party on!*

Katie Johnston (12)
Killingworth Middle School

SILLY BILLY

There was a young boy called Billy,
Who was always being so silly,
He would run down the streets,
And everyone who he meets,
Would shout, 'Oi, here comes silly Billy.'

Alex Pearson (13)
Killingworth Middle School

FOOTBALL, FOOTBALL

Football, football, what a wonderful game,
Football, football, it's anything but lame.
Strikers, strikers, scoring all the goals,
Strikers, strikers, in the net they leave holes.
Keepers, keepers, all over the place,
Keepers, keepers, sometimes a disgrace.
Defenders, defenders, we always blame them,
Defenders, defenders, for giving away a pen.
Midfielders, midfielders, sharp in their lances,
Midfielders, midfielders, create all the chances.
Referee, referee, blamed by the masses,
Referee, referee, where are your glasses?
Goals, goals, what a wonderful thing,
Goals, goals, the more you score, the more you win.
Grass, grass, all over the place,
Get a bad tackle it gets in your face.
Crowd, crowd, their voices still linger,
Score an own goal, they stick up their fingers.
Players, players, get loads of dosh,
When they miss sitters their mouth needs a wash.
Stadiums, stadiums, are a new generation,
Unfortunately their team heads for relegation.

Football, football, what a wonderful game!

Leon A Millar (12)
Killingworth Middle School

IS YOUR GIRLFRIEND . . . ?

Is your girlfriend funny?
Mine is.

Is your girlfriend helpful and friendly?
Mine is.

Is your girlfriend pretty and nicely dressed?
Mine is.

Is your girlfriend loving?
Mine is.

Does your girlfriend have a good chat with
You or her friends?
Mine does,

and is your girlfriend real . . .
mine isn't!

Michael Oldham (12)
Killingworth Middle School

WINTER FUN

Winter is one of the four seasons,
We love it so much and these are the reasons.

We have snowball fights and sledge races,
We have so much fun you can see it on our faces.

We build a snowman and put a carrot for its nose,
Then we go inside and warm our cold toes.

Rebecca Allan (11)
Killingworth Middle School

SPIDERS!

Running around trying to find me they are,
So far they've trapped me in a jar,
But when I escaped through a hole in the lid,
They nearly stood on me they did!

I feel very scared and alone,
But each time I make one they ruin my home,
I crawled into the garden, they let out the dog,
I scuttled into the kitchen, to meet the cat, Mog,
I've crawled around trying to find a home for me,
And maybe, just maybe a little company.

Ashleigh Donovan (11)
Killingworth Middle School

ONCE I SAW A MONSTER

Once I saw a monster
A scary sight it was.
Its skin green and flaky
Its nose was wet and flat.
The smell from it was disgusting,
Its hair dirty and scruff.
I never want to see that monster again
Because it smells enough!

Jonathan Cochrane
Killingworth Middle School

BUGS

Creepy crawlies, big and small,
Short and fat, thin and tall,
Some with six legs, some with four,
Some with a hundred, maybe more.

There is the caterpillar and the butterfly,
The ladybird and the dragonfly,
They live in the garden, in the house,
With the people and the mouse.

Below the bed, among the weed,
A dangerous life indeed.
They get flushed down the toilet,
And down the plug hole,
Hit by the newspaper,
Squished by a pole.

So they hide behind bottles,
And underneath the plug,
And as you can see,
It's tough to be a *bug!*

Emma Bryce (12)
Killingworth Middle School

THE MATCH HAIKU

See the crowd flood in
We know it's got to begin
Then the whistle goes.

Lee Rutherford (11)
Killingworth Middle School

I WISH . . .

I wish that there would be no more pollution,
Had I the power to make it happen,
I would stop all these oil spills, and petrol polluting the air.
I would stop all this if I could,
But I have nothing to save the world from pollution.
I have nothing but my voice to tell others why they should try and
Create a better world for all of us.

Kimberley Sahni (12)
Gosforth Central Middle School

I WISH TO TURN BACK TIME

Had I the time, if it was not too late,
To change my ever tragic fate.
If I could now go back in time,
I would alter my ill-fated crime.
But I, myself, have to forget,
The clock is ticking,
I can't help regret.

Jessie Waugh (12)
Gosforth Central Middle School

I WISH FOR POLLUTION'S END

Had I the ability to remove pollution,
to keep our air clean,
all the aerosols would disappear,
to let the world breathe.
But I am only me, no miracle worker like Jesus or God,
I have only my dreams, that one day may come true.

Kayleigh Slone (13) & Nicola Elliott (12)
Gosforth Central Middle School

I WISH THERE'D BE MORE POLICEMEN!

Had I the power to provide more policemen
guarding all the streets
I would be in a much safer place,
but I know most of all, I would be in a better place.
I have to do something,
but a child has no means of creating
such a place.

Sabrina Bhalla (12)
Gosforth Central Middle School

I WISH THERE WAS NO WAR

Had I the power of the people's voice,
The voice that pleads for no more war,
I would put an end to this horrible sight,
But I do not have the people's voice,
I have my wishes to bring peace to the world.

Richard Milburn & Paul Brown (12)
Gosforth Central Middle School

WORLD PEACE

Had I the power to create world peace,
I would liberate the world from war,
But I am only a child without power or influence,
I have just to think and dream of
A world with equality and peace.

Jack Bruce (12)
Gosforth Central Middle School

MY SISTER AND ME

First there was my sister,
Then there was me,
We were little devils,
My sister and me.

We ran through the house,
Up and down the street,
Said hello to strangers,
Everyone we meet.

At the age of nine,
I went out with her friends,
Out without my mummy,
For the very first time.

Followed her everywhere,
Like a cat to a mouse,
But now we just fight,
Like cat and dog.

I hope that my children,
Get on like we did,
Except for the fighting,
It's doing my head in!

Heather Slee (13)
Gosforth Central Middle School

THE BUTTERFLY

Suddenly and magically the chrysalis cracks,
Steadily, slowly the new-formed butterfly emerges.
Its crumpled wings and little head gradually appear,
Look, the shimmering creature's out!

It lies on its perch, drying its wings,
Then its first maiden flight in the summer breeze.
The butterfly's a flash of coloured, bright wings,
Sadly, now all too soon, the day becomes night.

Philippa Leith (12)
Gosforth Central Middle School

A REAL WORLD

I live in a real world with real people
By my side.
I live in peace and happiness with family
By my side.

I have a family who love me
And I love them back
I wonder what life would be like without love.
It would be full of sorrow and pain,
My family wouldn't be together without love,
And my life wouldn't be complete.

Happiness is a gift from above,
Without happiness the world would be a
Very sad place.
Lives are put together with love and happiness.
But what if someone were to take that away?
My life wouldn't be complete.

I live in a real world with real people
By my side.
I live in peace and happiness with family
By my side,
And no one can take that away from me.

Laura Scott (12)
Gosforth Central Middle School

ONE FATAL MOVE

One Sunday morning,
A day of hesitation
As the darkest enemy rode in,
For all that he knew it was going to be victory day,
As on the pitch
Every Sunday I would watch in despair,
As time went by,
Fifteen, thirty, forty-five minutes went,
They were winning
Two goals to nil,
Sixty, seventy-five minutes went,
Then, one sudden move,
And he was off like a limping bear
As the team looked in disbelief,
I didn't care for the match at that moment in time,
That one fatal move cost the day,
That was then and this is now,
He fights another day.

Craig Wilson (12)
Gosforth Central Middle School

I WISH I RULED THE STARS

Had I the power over the deep blue velvet orb,
Encrusted with silver stars,
I would keep those stars shining,
Not letting them dim,
But I am only an insignificant glint,
I have only the dreams of an aluminium silhouette,
Until my lustre ends.

Samantha Quearns (12)
Gosforth Central Middle School

MY FAMILY

My family, the largest piece of jigsaw to my life,
Without that piece, my life would be incomplete.
Mother, father, sister and grandparents,
Always by my side in everything I do,
Not only that but my role models too.

When I was troubled, my mind was but a haze,
My mother and father helped me accomplish the intractable mind maze.
From my first ride on a bike,
To my first day at school,
They were always there for me.

But maybe one day there will be a slight change,
As I will be independent and confident too.
My parents' eternal clock will eventually stop ticking,
And the happy times we shared will be nothing but past memories,
They won't always be there for me.

Kate Anderson (12)
Gosforth Central Middle School

THE POWER TO CHANGE THE EARTH

Had I the power to change the Earth,
I'd bring great beauty to every new birth.
No war and no hunger would happen again,
No plague and no famine would cause people pain.
Humans and creatures would live in peace,
Fighting and war would suddenly cease.
Peace would live on through countries and towns,
But I should help people who always feel down.

Mark Waite (12)
Gosforth Central Middle School

FAMILY LIFE

I look out of my window
And think of my life,
About what I have done,
And what is to come.

The houses resemble my family;
My family argues,
Whose family doesn't?
We have our ups and downs,
But mostly we get on.

The dark clouds resemble the bad times in life;
My sister is epileptic
Which is quite a worry,
And I really wish that
She'd get well in a hurry.

My mum is really kind
And would do anything for me,
But she really worries about my sister
Like the rest of the family.

My dad puts on a brave face,
But I know he's worried inside,
He tries to comfort my mum,
But there's no one there to comfort him.

I don't really understand,
I don't know what's going on,
But I try to stay happy and cheerful,
To keep everyone hanging on.

Caroline McGreevy (12)
Gosforth Central Middle School

LIFE

What is life?
Is life a game or just fun?
Life can't be long,
All life is, is a test.

We learn from life,
We learn from people,
If we don't learn,
Life is all but a waste.

When we are born the test begins,
The first step is just an obstacle,
The first word is just a hurdle,
School is a monster you must learn to defeat.

Life will end one day,
Everyone knows it.
Then heaven or hell will be
Your grade.

If you pass you will enjoy,
If you don't your life will wither away.

So work hard for your test.
Revise for Judgement Day.
Then maybe you won't have a big price
To pay.

Ahsan Shujaat (12)
Gosforth Central Middle School

GRANDAD

Grandad was in the Paras,
My mother told me that,
He broke his left leg badly.

A few years back he used to tell
Sad stories about the war,
Which made me think deeply of
How terrible it was for him.

Two years ago he passed away,
(In his sleep, happily.)

Today I feel I want them back,
Those long-lost stories he told,
I feel I want them back because,
They were special, until I die.

James Stephenson (12)
Gosforth Central Middle School

WORLD PEACE

Had I one wish,
I would wish for world peace,
For the world to be a much safer place,
But I am only living in a world
Of poverty and despair,
I have only my thoughts,
The hope and the belief,
That the world will be a
Much safer place.

Elizabeth Lawrence (12)
Gosforth Central Middle School

GRANDAD

His garden is like a jungle,
It is full of colourful plants,
He could remember every single name,
He could even spell them out.

He had a big pond full of fish,
He held my hand while I walked around,
He never let me fall in,
He watched my every move.

But now he's got a disease,
It's eating him up inside,
He's in and out of hospital,
It's like he's not alive.

It's me, who holds his hand,
I have to keep the garden,
I watch his every move,
But I know he's not right inside.

Sarah Elliott (12)
Gosforth Central Middle School

I WISH THE WORLD WAS A HANDFUL OF JOY

Had I the sun, the moon, the sky,
Perfect picture, lined with gold,
Like love, as I see it.
Happiness, joy, a perfect new land,
I would wish upon the heavens,
Just to have you in my heart,
But I don't have the sun, or the heavens, or the sky,
I have love of mine, to offer you and I.

Freya Brown (12)
Gosforth Central Middle School

MEMORIES OF GRANDMA

I used to love going to my grandma's,
Getting sweets and going to the park,
But now I find myself alone
And sitting in the dark.

I used to love going to my grandma's,
Getting presents, buns and cakes,
But at night when I go to bed,
It just keeps me awake.

I used to love going to my grandma's,
Getting all hyped up and mad,
But now all those fun times
Seem to be sad.

I think about my grandpa,
Everywhere and anywhere but,
When I think about it seriously,
It breaks my heart in two,
Because now I know he's going to go too.

Simon Beavers (12)
Gosforth Central Middle School

I WISH FOR NO POVERTY

Had I a lot of wealth,
All the money in the world,
I would give a little to everyone,
But alas I only have a little share.
I will just have to wait
For my dream to become reality,
And poverty to reduce.

Hollie Purves (12)
Gosforth Central Middle School

Old Waters

I watch my elders on the gunwale,
The wind whistling over the beam,
The sails are full and sheets are tough.

The helm sits royal on the stern,
As the crew move around the deck,
And me as a mere worker, turning
Winches and hauling in sheets.
But as I watch I can see my king
Grow older and as his throne
Shall fall and I will rebel and become king.

The rolling waters of the sea,
Crash and smash all around me,
I'm still working here, turning
Winches and hauling in sheets.

Now I'm king! And the crew is small,
I sit on the quarter watching the world go by.
Then after this dream, I see my elders on the gunwale
And the wind whistling over the beam . . .

Tom Somerville (12)
Gosforth Central Middle School

I WISH FOR THE WAR TO STOP!

Had I the power to rule the land,
No more war or unkind in hand,
No more death by sword or fight,
No more sights too hard to see.
I would give my peace to stop it all,
But I haven't the power to rule the land,
I have only my dreams to stop it all!

Christine Blair (12)
Gosforth Central Middle School

ME, MY FAMILY AND OTHER THINGS

Me, is a word to describe things,
So I'll use it to describe me,
A happy baby sitting in the sun,
A little boy playing with toys.

Me, a boy starting school today,
A youth downtown without a care.
A young man flying a jet plane,
Enough about me, my family.

Them, is a word to describe things,
So I'll use it to paint families.
My family has four people,
A mum, a dad, and two children.

Mum is kind, helpful and patient,
Dad cracks bad jokes and thinks he's old,
The little brother is alright,
But the big brother is great fun.

Feelings, is a word to describe things,
So I'll use it to describe mine.
I know that time passes, but why?
I wonder how we'd survive without?

Do I think there would be chaos,
Or do I think life would be still?
To be honest I don't know yet,
But I may well find out later.

Images, is a word to describe things,
So I'll use it to describe mine,
I see myself going to school,
I see myself leaving the school.

Sometimes I see myself playing,
On the happy machine (PlayStation),
I'm not at school in the holidays.
              I wish!

Peter Bloxsom (12)
Gosforth Central Middle School

THE HOPE FOR A CONKER

In autumn, when the colours change,
The conkers start to come again,
Some grow big and some grow small,
But in the end I love them all.

Every year I see the tree,
With the big, green conkers hanging there,
Every day I tried my best,
To get the conkers from the tree.

The more I tried, the harder it got,
The tree was just too high for me,
Until, one day, I threw a stick,
And down came falling from the tree,
The biggest conker I will ever see.

In my hand I held the conker,
Still protected by its spiky armour,
I gently opened it,
But to my disappointment,
It was not the smooth brown conker
I was hoping for.

I will now have to wait yet another year,
Until I will get my dream conker.

Fiona Urwin (12)
Gosforth Central Middle School

WORKER

My father works with an aeroplane,
His hands are oily black,
Between the wings and engine,
His plane stood still at his clicking wrench.

An expert. He stood on the wing,
And fixed silver nuts on top,
The nuts turned with strength,
On the nose that he would touch. It was fixed
In a matter of seconds.

Of the wheels that go round,
And back into the garage,
Wings turned up so it would fit,
Mapping the size exactly.

I stumbled into the plane,
Sometimes onto the floor,
I sometimes rode down the emergency slide,
Dipping down 'til I hit the floor.

I wanted to fly the plane one day,
Up into the sky, wearing the hat.
All I ever did was watch.

I was a nuisance, tripping, falling,
Talking always, but today it is
My father who keeps stumbling,
Always.

Chris Foley (12)
Gosforth Central Middle School

PAINTINGS

Dramatic scenes painted in my head,
But I can't paint, I'll watch instead.

I hear a soft humming from a room down the hall,
I walk in to see my father, oil paints and all.
I see the painted canvas with colours of many different shades.
Painting a breathtaking image,
Madness expressed in patterns.

How does he do it? Is it hard?
Maybe he could show me, or maybe not!

I see Dunstanburgh Castle, about to face a storm,
Its stonework looking mighty strong,
It reminds me of a battle, who will win?

I see a gigantic rock, standing all alone,
The sea swirling around it, trapped from beckoning land.

They amaze me, these images do,
But all of them are not real.
They're painted on canvas,
By my father!

He stops painting, there's a grin on his face,
He shows me his latest design,
A silhouetted sunset on the Borders hills.
I don't need to paint like him, I have my own skills,
That he follows me in.

Dramatic scenes painted in my head, but I paint with pen instead.

Rachel Dawson (12)
Gosforth Central Middle School

GRANDFATHER

Helping him in the garden,
Every little thing I got wrong.
He always came to the rescue though,
Like a fireman putting out a fire.

He never forgot anyone's name,
Always remembered where people were.
Taking me home in his car,
Laughing at the smallest joke.

I admired his garden.
Looked up to him,
I found him very reliable,
Always there when I made mistakes.

But now he never remembers names.
Can't remember when he went or when he came.
I'm the one in the garden doing the work,
He's the one watching and admiring.

Rebecca Elliott (12)
Gosforth Central Middle School

I WISH THE WORLD WAS A PERFECT DREAM

Had I embroidered silk and candyfloss clouds,
Golden gates, sparkling in perfect sunlight,
Love which was true and never burnt out,
Happiness which was there forever and ever,
I would take you there, where the picture was unspoilt,
But I spoilt it by ruining the love,
I have told you my wish of happiness,
So you can share the same perfect dream.

Christina Snowden (12)
Gosforth Central Middle School

MY PARENTS' JOB

C&B Carpets is our name,
Supplying carpets is our aim.
There're rugs galore and much, much more
And wooden flooring for your floor.
With tape in hand my dad does the measures,
You can come in the shop and browse at your leisure,
Where meeting my mum would give you great pleasure.
Sitting at her desk waiting for the phone to ring,
She'll answer your enquiry on anything.
After five they close the shutter,
To arrive home to a big mess and clutter.
She starts again to make our tea,
Whilst we are watching our favourite, MTV.

Jason Ford (12)
Gosforth Central Middle School

ME AND MY MUM

Me and my mum used to fight,
Fight all day and every night,
But now we don't fight and fight,
Because there is not anything
That we should fight about.

Now we sit down and watch TV,
Have a good laugh at what I say,
I wish you would forgive me,
And I hope we can start again,
And she forgave me.

Suzanne Eaddie (12)
Gosforth Central Middle School

LOOKING INTO THE FUTURE

I look out at the sky and see,
The birds cheeping and the flowers blooming,
All wonderful creations our Lord God made,
He made me tough like concrete and strong as steel.

I was the twinkle of the stars,
Approximately thirteen years,
Shining bright, like the golden light.

I came to Earth, not knowing how,
All I know is I have loving parents,
Who love me and support me,
Which I most truly cherish.

When I see the world in motion,
Seeing everyone at work,
I think of my dream job, and me,
What would I like to be?

In life I have doubts whether
I'm good enough for people,
Or maybe death comes into conscience,
Sometimes it's hard not to think about it.

I think about the near future,
So exciting but not quite yet,
Waiting for joy and happiness,
To spring out of my face.

What will Mum be like?
Will she feel like an eighteen year old again?
Or will she start to knit or bake?
I don't know.

As I'm young, I think of all the fun,
And laughs I'm going to have,
I feel it's like a Christmas present,
Waiting to be opened.
But it's best to leave them wrapped,
So that you'll never be disappointed,
Well, these are my thoughts,
Tell me yours.

Annie Messropian (12)
Gosforth Central Middle School

MEMORIES

My Nana Joyce is very nice,
She is just like my friend,
I never thought she would go and leave me.

The morning I found out she had,
I was very upset.

I will never forget her, or the morning.

I felt as if it was a dream,
Deep down I knew the truth.

Were they lying?
No. They would not lie about something like this.
Is it some kind of joke, or what?

I remember when she used to take me out,
I never thought those days would go.

Will I awake from this nightmare?

I miss her so very much,
More than words can say.

Kirsty Knowles (12)
Gosforth Central Middle School

MY GRANDPA AND A GUITAR

My grandpa strummed his grand guitar
He strummed and played all through the day.

He can play all sorts of tunes,
Like Elvis Presley's *Blue Suede Shoes.*

My grandpa bought me a guitar,
It was covered in colours that melted into each other.

I wished I could play as well as him.

I hoped,
I prayed all and every day,
That I was as good as he was today.

I am not a guitarist like my grandpa, I can't strum
And play like a summer's day.

I am a girl recording all my thoughts and dreams.

I hope someday I'll look back and say;
I can strum and play.

Jessica Rachael Mills (12)
Gosforth Central Middle School

I WISH FOR WORLD PEACE

Had I one wish I could make,
The power of one single wish,
I would pray for world peace,
But I do not have a magical power,
I have just the hunger for a wish,
To remove all suffering and distress,
And to replace it with happiness, comfort and love.

Glen Heckels (13)
Gosforth Central Middle School

MY GRANDFATHER

My grandfather is a hard working man,
Day and night, night and day,
He works on his little farm, digging away,
In boiling weather, it is never cold.

He tosses, turns and folds the soil,
And plants the seeds neatly in rows.
Now all he needs is rain to help them grow.

He waits and waits for the rain to come.
In the hot, hot summer not a drop of rain
Fell on his land.

If this was me or if this was you,
We would call it a day,
Sell the farm and move away.

But no, not my grandfather!
Through thick and thin he was determined,
He never gave in.
He never said no, he was never defeated,
No matter what his task,
It would be completed.

Now he is too old to dig and plant,
He sits in his armchair with a grin on his face,
And pride in his heart,
As he watches his son work,
Day and night, night and day,
Happily content with digging away.

Nadia Bailey (12)
Gosforth Central Middle School

ADMIRATION

I admire her with all of my mind,
She sits for hours on end, hard at work,
Stone hard fingers press down on the block keys,
Her eyes move steadily across the screen,
Just like a falcon watching its own prey.

It is the way she can switch on to work,
It used to puzzle me. Why does she work?
But now I know why she does what she does,
She works for the family that she loves.

Hopefully someday I will be like her,
Working very hard for my family,
My kids will watch me in admiration,
And maybe they will be able to say,
I admire her with all of my mind.

Victoria Graham (12)
Gosforth Central Middle School

I WISH FOR THE MONEY

Had I the wealth to give,
For folk like us who need to live.
For the elderly and the homeless,
I would share my wish to make their dreams come true.
I have no money or power,
But I can give my heart and soul,
To secure, comfort and care for those in need.

Katy Appleton (12)
Gosforth Central Middle School

MY GRANDAD

My grandad is a jolly chap,
Who wears a chequered scarf and cap.
His garden is where he likes to be,
With all his lovely flowers to see.
With bulbs to plant and seeds to sow,
He pulls out the weeds with his jolly big hoe!
He sits in his garden whenever he can,
GM food he would like to ban.
When indoors he likes to read,
And do his crosswords with great speed.
He really is an intelligent man,
Who tries to help us whenever he can.
He walks with a stick so cannot run,
But he's kind and caring and very good fun.

Ashleigh Weldon (12)
Gosforth Central Middle School

A POEM FOR PEACE

I wish that all the world had peace
Had I the power to heal
And end the awful bad ordeal,
And then all countries would talk,
And laugh and not just fight and kill.

I would heal the wounded and end the strife,
But I am not the one to heal the sick.
I have the dream that I still hope
And wish to live and love to care,
And make the world a
Better place.

Geraint Goodfellow (12)
Gosforth Central Middle School

PARENTS

My father works all day, and
Mother does the same as well.
In a factory he does,
In a library you know.

A master he is anything he can make,
She knows all the books from A-Z.
Tanks, tanks, tanks, that is what he makes,
Books, books, books, is what she does now.

I don't want to work in a factory,
I don't want to work in a library,
I am undecided in what I want to do,
I will just have to wait and see.

Michael Hedley (12)
Gosforth Central Middle School

PAST AND PRESCIENT

Memories flow from ear to toe,
Prancing and dancing around.

Laughing and singing as time went by,
Under the thick daunting sky,
Looking for signs with Preston on,
Jumping with excitement, nearly there.

Grandma and family waiting for us,
Mum growing sleepy, as time went by.

All is different, Grandma's not here,
But still excitement runs through me,
Memories still alive.

Charlotte Elder (12)
Gosforth Central Middle School

SURVIVORS

My family goes out,
I'm left all alone,
How do I take my mind off being lonely?
I'll think of something else.

I'll think of survivors,
My grandparents,
I'll think of World War II,
I'll think of survivors.

My grandparents survived this,
The bombs, the guns, the grief,
Loved ones are lost,
But, thank God, they survived.

I'll think of alarms and explosions,
Rubble lying on the ground,
My grandparents survived this,
But how, I don't know.

I'll think of another alarm,
That of an ambulance,
My grandfather can't survive this,
This is a heart attack.

My family go out,
I'm left all alone,
I'll think of my grandmother,
She feels a different kind of loneliness.

I think to the future,
And what it holds for me,
Will I survive,
Or will I cough, choke, and die?

Michael Owens (12)
Gosforth Central Middle School

DAY AT THE BEACH

The sun had climbed to the top of the sky
And had dried out the last of the morning dew.
As the faint lapping sound of the sea,
Slowly covered the pebbled-covered sand.

As the first family arrive at the beach,
And are looking for an adventure,
As they pick the best spot on the beach,
And set the rug out for the picnic.

But my grandma and grandpa can only watch,
They watch in jealousy,
As they are both too old to go to the beach,
As the sun disappears over the horizon,
And another day goes by.

Harry Robson (12)
Gosforth Central Middle School

A FLOWERING FANTASY

Lying awake in bed at night,
Brings me thoughts of much delight.

Like a Roman candle my dreams cascade,
Into a magical parade.

The eternal beauty of the scene,
This paradise must be a dream.

The sun is setting beneath the trees,
Vibrant colours of autumn leaves.

A wonderful world blooms like a bud,
I would make it real if I only could.

Janie McCullough (12)
Gosforth Central Middle School

MARROWS

My dad puts marrow in everything,
Grown in the allotment,
Usually half a metre long.

Marrow stuffed with lamb mince,
Marrow with ginger soup,
But what really bugs me most,
Is marrow straight from the root.

My family seem to like it,
I suppose the soup is all right,
Tastes like leek and potato,
(Which I think is quite nice).

But the lamb and marrow is unbearable,
We've had it once or twice,
He's been digging all summer,
And there's still more to come.

Michael Brown (12)
Gosforth Central Middle School

I WISH FOR PEACE IN THE WORLD

Had I the power to stop the wars,
And open quiet, peaceful doors.
I would change the way other countries act,
I, myself have pleasant thoughts packed.
I have thoughts about the world,
Some day they might just be unfurled.
To proclaim a glorious peace,
Which may never, never cease.

Nicola Torrance (12)
Gosforth Central Middle School

WOODWORKER

Grandad was a joiner when I was young,
Working on houses with his tools and hands.
He'd come to our house in late afternoon,
His hands black-dusted with the dirt and grime.
Grandad worked throughout the day and with a will,
Said he enjoyed his job, which I believe was true.
I thought no one could match his skill with wood.
His blackened hands were like a part of him,
Like hair or eyes, and I loved them as him.

My grandad could create all kinds of things,
A magic wonderland from shapeless wood!
The shapes would interlock effortlessly,
And gracefully build as I watched there, amazed.
I dreamed that someday I would follow him, and
Be as skilful with the blocks of wood.
But my hands were not made to hold a saw,
Or turn a piece of timber on a lathe.

And yet I match his skill another way,
Creating magic with colourful words.
My words together glimpse a fairyland,
A graceful work, imagination's child.

I may not be as clever with my hands,
But I can lay a starting point today.
I build and interlock fragments of life,
Shaping the future in a special way.

Frances L Weightman (13)
Gosforth Central Middle School

FRUIT

The summer is here
The sun shines
The fruit of summer grows

How nice the fruit looks
When you pick it fresh off a bush or tree
The juices the flavours
Oh! What a delight

The strawberries are red
The apples are green
Fruit of the summer
Please let the birds leave you clean

My dad used to pick fruit
So did my mum
Now I do the fruit picking
Because it is so fun

The fun it used to be as
The bags used to burst
Juices ran everywhere
But that's okay if you are dying of thirst

In the future will people still pick?
Or will it be all genetically modified
I sure hope not
Because nothing can beat fresh fruit

But when the winter comes
The fruit starts to go
But do not fret
As it will be back next summer
Or will it?

Alan Spodick (13)
Gosforth Central Middle School

THE LIFE OF A ROSE

Among the wild thornberries grows
A pretty flower, a wild rose.

As it waves about in the breeze,
And gently shimmers in my eyes,
A vain young shoot, a beautiful haze.

Its outer petals are brightly coloured
As yellow as a lion's fur,
Yet inside the gentle colours
Are as soft as a new-born kitten,
Yet the body is quite different,
A slim, stiff pine green stem, scattered with thorns.

Each day I pass and search for it,
And each day I am rewarded,
Each day it grows and blossoms more,
And so grows richer and richer.

Then I came and started my search,
With nothing different about me,
Apart from the feeling inside of myself,
For I was claiming my bounty.

And soon I found that wild rose,
Among the wild thornberries there,
Swaying about the light breeze.

I pluck it away from its roots,
And run quickly home to show off my prize.
I lay it on the window sill,
Its beauty captured in the sun.

A few days later, I come down
To throw something in the rubbish,
One closer look shows that it is
My wild rose, all dry like a desert,
Its beauty gone, its stem is shrivelled,
Its petals like an old man's skin,
If only I had not plucked it.

Its time has passed, I killed it off,
My gentle rose's life was cruel.

Ellen Andersen (12)
Gosforth Central Middle School

YOU

You are my inspiration
You will inspire me
You have inspired me
Yet how can I inspire you?

You show me all I see
You've shown me all I've seen
You will show me all I will see
Yet what can I show you?

You gave me all I have
You've given me all I've got
You'll give me all I will ever have
Yet what can I give you back?

When I am young as are you
As I grow you grow with me
As I am as you are, you will be old
And as I am old you will be no more.

Joseph Coady-Stemp (13)
Gosforth Central Middle School

DAD

I fell down off the banisters,
He caught me, he caught me.
I fell into a swimming pool,
Sinking, sinking,
He reached in and pulled me out.

He taught me how to swim,
He taught me how to run,
Making models and gliders,
We always had great fun.

I fell down off the banisters,
He caught me, he caught me.
I fell into a swimming pool,
Sinking, sinking,
He reached in and pulled me out.

Stories of Bilbo Baggins,
Stig and Just William too.
Stories of far-away places,
And a bear named Winnie the Pooh.

I fell down off the banisters,
He caught me, he caught me.
I fell into a swimming pool,
Sinking, sinking,
He reached in and pulled me out.

Camping, bike rides and fishing,
Football in the park.
He was always there to comfort me,
When I was afraid of the dark.

I fell down off the banisters,
He caught me, he caught me.
I fell into a swimming pool,
Sinking, sinking,
He reached in and pulled me out.

Nick Appleton (13)
Gosforth Central Middle School

BEING BORED

Nagging, nagging, all day long,
My father for a thing to do,
All day long, day and night,
Something to do.

Grandad painted, I was bored,
Bored stiff like a statue made from stone,
Picking up a brush to paint,
Slapping paint all over the slate.

Making a model was my uncle,
Very skilled, like a sparrow making a nest,
I was bored, watching,
Snap, like a gun firing, a piece snaps.

Cakes, cakes, was my auntie making,
Yum, yum, icing on top,
'Can I help make the top?'
Smudge, my thumb goes through the cake like a knife through butter.

Being bored,
It is not nice to be bored,
Nothing to do all the time,
For being bored is not nice.

Simon Fox (12)
Gosforth Central Middle School

HAD I THE POWER . . .

Had I the power to control the world,
Every man, woman, boy and girl,
Every mountain, valley and river so deep,
The sea, the sky and the sun,
I would put an end to all poverty,
Homelessness and despair,
But I am just a child, with no power or influence,
But I have dreams of a world of peace.

Adam Beaney & Munzir El-Amin (12)
Gosforth Central Middle School